Swans

and Other Swimming Birds

Concept and Product Development: Editorial Options, Inc.
Series Designer: Karen Donica
Book Author: Steven A. Horak

For information on other World Book
products, visit us at our Web site at
http://www.worldbook.com

For information on sales to schools and
libraries in the United States, call 1-800-975-3250.

For information on sales to schools and
libraries in Canada, call 1-800-837-5365.

World Book, Inc.
233 N. Michigan Ave.
Chicago, IL 60601

Library of Congress Cataloging-in-Publication Data

Swans and other swimming birds.
        p. cm. -- (World Book's animals of the world)
    ISBN 0-7166-1217-8 -- ISBN 0-7166-1211-9 (set)
    1. Swans--Juvenile literature. 2. Anatidae--Juvenile literature. [1. Swans.
    2. Waterfowl.] I. World Book, Inc. II. Series.

    QL508.A2 S925 2001
    598.418--dc21   2001017525

Printed in Singapore

1 2 3 4 5 6 7 8 9 05 04 03 02 01

World Book's Animals of the World

Swans
and Other Swimming Birds

How do I show off?

World Book, Inc.
A Scott Fetzer Company
Chicago

Contents

Why do people mistake me for a parrot?

What do I use for brakes?

Who chatters while eating?

What Are Swimming Birds?

As you can probably guess, swimming birds are birds that swim. Swans are swimming birds. So are ducks and geese. Puffins, storm-petrels, and loons are also swimming birds.

Some swimming birds, such as swans, ducks, and geese, are closely related. Others are not so closely related. Still, all swimming birds are alike in that they spend most of their lives near water.

Like all birds, swimming birds have feathers. And they have bills and feet. But the feathers, feet, and bills of swimming birds have special features for life in and near the water. Swans, for example, have waterproof feathers and webbed feet for swimming. They have flat bills for eating water plants.

Whooper swans

Where in the World Do Swans Live?

Swimming birds can be found on every continent—including Antarctica. Swans, however, live on just five continents. These swimming birds prefer places that have mild or cool climates. Swans do not live in Africa, where the temperatures get very hot. And they do not live in Antarctica, where temperatures are too cold.

There are seven species, or kinds, of swans. Four species live in the Northern Hemisphere, and three species live in the Southern Hemisphere.

Where a swan lives tells you a little bit about it. For example, swans that live in the Northern Hemisphere have only white feathers. Swans that live in South America have either black wing tips or black necks. Australian swans are nearly all black. Northern swans are also larger than southern swans.

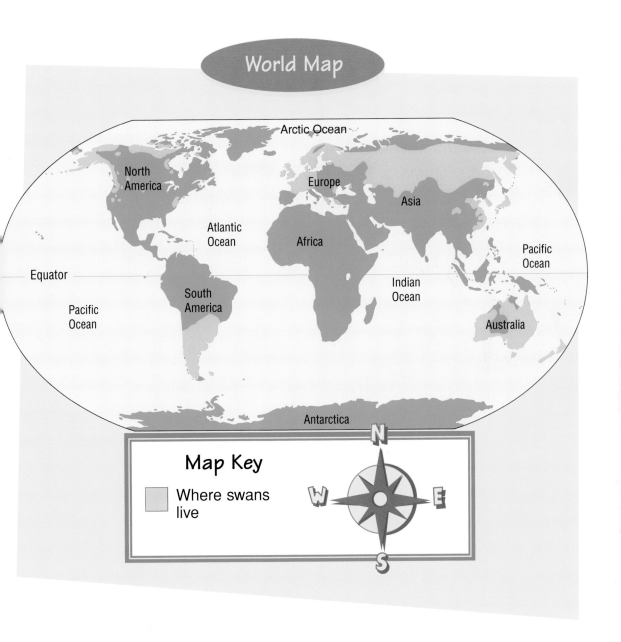

World Map

Arctic Ocean

North America

Europe

Asia

Atlantic Ocean

Africa

Pacific Ocean

Equator

Indian Ocean

South America

Pacific Ocean

Australia

Antarctica

Map Key

Where swans live

N

W E

S

What Makes Swans Good Swimmers?

Swans have many features that make them good swimmers. They have webbed feet, air sacs, waterproof feathers, and widely spaced legs.

Like most birds, swans have four toes on each foot. But swans also have webs of skin between three of their toes. To swim, they use their webbed feet like paddles.

Swans have air sacs connected to their lungs. They also have hollow bones. The air sacs and hollow bones act like life preservers. They help keep swans afloat.

Under their feathers, swans also have downy coats. The down traps pockets of air. This keeps the swan warm. It also helps the swan float.

Finally, a swan's legs are set wide apart and far back on its body. This helps the bird keep its balance and paddle through the water.

Black-necked swan

11

When Do Graceful Swans Look Clumsy?

Swans are very graceful fliers. They flap their big, strong wings with powerful beats. They fly with their necks stretched out and their legs tucked in. But swans are large and heavy birds. Like this mute swan, they have trouble taking off and landing. That's when swans look clumsy!

When swans want to fly, they need to gather up speed to help them take off. For this, swans need a runway. The runway is usually a long stretch of land or water. Swans pat across the water, flapping their wings as fast as they can. At first, they look clumsy. But once they are in the air, they can fly very well.

Landings can be tricky for swans. This may be why many swans choose to land on the water. To land, swans spread out their wings and their tail feathers to catch the air and slow down. Then they put their feet forward and use them as brakes to touch down.

Mute swan

 13

What Do Swans Eat?

Swans eat mostly water plants. And they eat all the parts—leaves, stems, roots, and seeds. Swans eat plants found on the surface of the water, along the shore, and under the water. Young swans eat small animals, such as insects, worms, and tiny fish. In winter, swans may come on land to feed.

Swans use their long necks to reach underwater plants. To do this, a swan puts its neck under the water and upends, or raises its tail into the air. When a swan upends, it can reach down about 3 feet (1 meter) under the water.

A swan has a wide, flat bill with tiny, teethlike fringes along the edge. The bill is good for biting and tearing water plants. Swans open and close their bills quickly to squeeze water from their food. The fringes trap the food and let the water drain out.

Mute swan

How Do Swans Care for Their Feathers?

Swans care for their feathers in different ways. First, they take a lot of baths. They also preen, or use their bills to care for their feathers.

To bathe, swans may hold their wings open and dive underwater. Then they come up and roll along the surface of the water. Swans dry off by flapping their wings and shaking their bodies.

Swans spend a lot of time preening. When swans preen, they use their bills to straighten and rearrange their feathers. They use their bills to remove any insects from their feathers. And they use their bills to waterproof their feathers.

How do swans waterproof their feathers? A swan has a gland at the base of its tail that makes oil. The swan uses its bill to spread this oil over its feathers. The oil waterproofs the feathers.

Mute swan preening

Why Are Swans Sometimes Grounded?

Swans aren't grounded because they get into trouble! When swans are grounded, it means that they can't fly. This happens when swans molt, or shed their old feathers and grow new ones. If you look closely at the swans in this picture, you can see where they have shed their feathers.

Swans molt because their feathers wear out and need to be replaced. Swans usually molt once a year, during the summer months. With some species of swans, the males and females molt at different times. First the female molts. Then the male molts.

The molt lasts about six weeks. During this time, the swan cannot fly. But it can still swim. So molting swans stay close to the water. This makes it easier to find food and to escape from enemies.

Molting swans

Where Do Swans Go in Winter?

During the winter, many swans migrate, or travel long distances. They leave before the rivers and lakes freeze. Migrating swans fly to warmer climates or to places where they can find more food. Other swans do not migrate at all. They live by bodies of water that don't freeze.

Some swans travel to the seashore where the water is salty. The food is often salty, too. Swans have special salt glands that help get rid of extra salt. The salt comes out the swan's nostrils in a liquid like tears.

Swans may migrate more than 1,000 miles (1,600 kilometers). To prepare for this flight, a swan eats a lot of food. It stores the food as fat. The stored fat is like a fuel tank. It gives the swan the energy to fly long distances without stopping.

Migrating swans travel in family groups or in flocks. They usually fly in clear weather and use the sun or stars to guide them.

Whooper swans
migrating

Do Swans Mate for Life?

Swans usually do mate for life. But there are times when a swan does take a new mate. A swan may take a new mate if its partner gets lost or dies.

Swans choose mates when they are 2 to 3 years old. A swan begins its courtship by displaying, or showing off, to another swan. Swans display while facing each other. They dip and turn their heads. Swans may also "kiss" bills. When swans kiss, their necks form a heart shape.

Many swan pairs set up territories. A pair picks a territory where there is a lot of food and a safe place to build a nest. Swans defend their territories fiercely. They fight off an intruder by bumping it and hitting it with their wings. When the intruder leaves, the swan pair celebrates. They call loudly and face each other with raised wings.

Mute swans

Where Do Swans Build Their Nests?

All swans build their nests near water. Some build nests on the ground. Others build nests on plants floating on the water. Swans may also patch up a nest they used the year before.

Swans nest in the spring or early summer. The cob, or male swan, usually chooses the place and gathers the materials. He passes grass, twigs, and other plants to the pen, or female swan. The pen uses the plants to build a nest that may be more than 9 feet (3 meters) wide.

After laying her eggs, a pen sits on the eggs to incubate them, or keep them warm. The cob stays close by to guard the nest. Sometimes, a cob sits on the nest while the pen feeds.

After 30 to 35 days, tiny cheeps can be heard from inside the eggs. One by one, the baby swans hatch. The babies are called cygnets *(SIHG nihts)*.

Mute swan
with cygnets

Are Swans Ever Ugly Ducklings?

Some people think cygnets look like ugly ducklings. But if they do, it's not for very long. At first, the young cygnets are wet and scrawny looking. Then they dry off and become tiny balls of fluffy down.

When cygnets hatch, they weigh about 6 ounces (170 grams). That's about the same weight as a baseball. But an adult swan can weigh up to 26 pounds (12 kilograms). That is much larger than any duckling can grow.

After a day, cygnets can follow their parents into the water. They already know how to swim. But they won't be able to fly for 7 to 20 weeks. Until then, their parents swim or walk with them. Some swans even carry their young on their backs!

Black-necked swan
with cygnet

How Do Swans Care for Their Cygnets?

Cygnets grow more slowly than other swimming birds do. They need their parents for a longer time, too. Their parents help them find food and stay safe.

A few days after hatching, cygnets are ready for their first meal. Their parents help by pulling up underwater plants. Soon, cygnets are able to peck at water plants and insects on their own.

During the day, cygnets stay close to their parents. If a cygnet wanders off, a parent calls to it. And cygnets call to their parents if they need help. At night, cygnets sleep in the nest, safe and warm under their mother's wings.

Cygnets stay with their parents for about a year or two. This gives young swans time to learn such things as migration routes. Some swans stay with their parents until they are ready to choose mates of their own.

Black swan
with cygnets

How Do Trumpeter Swans Sound Off?

Trumpeter swans sound off with trumpetlike calls. How do they do this? A trumpeter swan has a very long neck. Inside the neck is a long trachea *(TRAY kee uh),* or windpipe. The trachea is so long that it even winds around the trumpeter's chest bone. It lets a trumpeter swan make its deep, hornlike calls. Trumpeter swans are the loudest of all swimming birds.

Pairs of trumpeter swans set up large territories. They need their loud calls to stay in touch with each other. Their calls are also a way to say: "Stay out of our territory!"

Swans are very vocal birds. The trumpeter swan, the whistling swan, and the whooper swan are all named for their calls. So you might think that the mute swan is mute, or silent. But even mute swans hiss, snort, and give off trumpetlike notes.

Trumpeter swan

Who Says "Hello" with a Honk?

Swans trumpet, whistle, and whoop. But geese honk to say "hello." Like swans, geese are very vocal. They, too, have long necks, webbed feet, and waterproof feathers. But geese are much smaller than most swans. Large geese weigh only around 9 pounds (4 kilograms).

The goose you see here is one of the noisiest species of geese. When a white-fronted goose flies, it has a high, musical call that sounds a bit like laughter—*lyo-lyok, lyo-lyok.* This call is so special that the goose can be identified by it. Some people even call white-fronted geese "laughing geese."

Like swans, geese use different calls for different reasons. One honk is a greeting. Another is a warning. Another signals that it is time for the flock to move on. Some geese have at least 10 different calls, each 1 for a different reason.

Greater white-fronted goose

Do Geese Make Good Lawn Mowers?

Geese feed on land much more than swans do. But barnacle geese don't just eat grass—they seem to mow right through it. They can clip grass at hundreds of snips a minute!

Two things help geese forage, or feed, on land. First, a goose's legs are close to the front of its body. This helps the goose walk comfortably on land. Second, a goose's bill is shaped like a triangle, with sharp notches along the edges. The notches help a goose cut through dry grass and other land plants.

Geese gather in family groups and large flocks to forage. Barnacle geese chatter when they forage. They give off sharp barks and yelps. And they compete for food. Geese in the middle of the flock often move to the edge to reach grassier spots.

Barnacle geese

Why Do Canada Geese Fly in Formation?

Canada geese fly in the shape of a V when they migrate. Many other swimming birds use this formation, too. It probably saves energy. It also allows birds to stay together and still see where they are flying.

How does a V-formation save energy? As the geese fly, the birds at the front of the V create upward air currents. The air currents help keep the rest of the flock up. This means that the birds at the back don't have to work so hard to fly. They use less energy.

Like other migrating birds, Canada geese take turns leading the formation. When the leader gets tired, it drops from the front of the V. Another goose then becomes the leader.

Canada geese

Which Geese Are Not Geese at All?

Pygmy *(PIHG mee)* geese are not geese. These swimming birds are actually ducks.

You may think that pygmy geese are as big as geese. But they are really the smallest of all ducks! In fact, an adult pygmy goose may weigh less than 7 ounces (200 grams). That's about the same weight as a newborn swan!

Like other ducks, pygmy geese have shorter necks and wings than swans and geese. But pygmy geese have very short wings—even for ducks. They have to flap their wings very quickly to fly.

Even though they are ducks, pygmy geese do have bills shaped like triangles. That's unusual for a duck!

Pygmy goose

How Is a Mallard Like a Swan?

Mallards, like swans, are dabblers. Dabblers are swimming birds that eat water plants and sift through mud to find food. A mallard's bill is like a swan's. The bill is flat and wide, with teethlike fringes along the edges to trap food and let water drain out.

A mallard is a medium-sized duck that weighs around 2 pounds (1 kilogram). Most drakes, or male ducks, have bright-colored feathers. Drake mallards are known for their shiny green heads and necks. They use their bright feathers to attract mates. Female mallards are mostly brown. This helps them blend into the surroundings when sitting on a nest or caring for ducklings.

Mallards

Which Ducks Have Whiskers?

Mandarin ducks have whiskers, just as cats do. But a mandarin's whiskers are very different from a cat's. A drake's bright orange whiskers are made of tiny feathers that hang from the sides of its head. Female mandarins also have feathery whiskers, but they are not colored brightly.

Drake mandarins also have a special set of feathers that look like sails. Can you see the sail in this picture?

What do mandarin ducks do with their special feathers? Like swans, mandarins display to attract mates. Drakes puff out their whiskers and sails to attract females.

Mandarin duck

Which Duck Has a Hood?

The hooded merganser *(muhr GAN suhr)* has a crest made of feathers. When the feathers lie flat, they look like hair. But when the feathers are raised, they look like a hood.

Both male and female mergansers have hoods. But a male's hood is larger and fuller. Males raise their hoods often. They raise their hoods to attract females. They may also raise their hoods when they are excited or in danger.

Like swans, hooded mergansers are good swimmers, but they are also good divers. They dive beneath the water to catch fish. Mergansers have long, thin bills with teethlike edges for grasping fish.

Hooded merganser

Who Is King of the North?

The king eider *(EYE duhr)* is a duck that lives in the Arctic. It lives farther north than most swimming birds. This makes it King of the North!

Being King of the North is not easy. The Arctic is a cold place with lots of snow and ice. But the king eider is built for the cold. This duck has a thick layer of down under its outer feathers. The down helps keep the king eider from getting cold.

All species of eiders are famous for their down. People use eider down to make pillows, quilts, and coats. In some places, people raise common eiders on farms. Female eiders line their nests with down to warm their eggs. The farmer collects the down from the nests. So what do the females do? They reline the nests! That keeps everyone happy.

King eider

Where Do Torrent Ducks Live?

Most swimming birds live near lakes, ponds, and oceans. But torrent ducks live on white-water rivers. Here, the water moves so quickly over rocks that it looks white and foamy.

Life in such fast waters isn't easy. Torrent ducks have big, strong webbed feet that help. They can grip slippery river rocks without falling. Their body shape and strong feet help them swim in the river currents.

Torrent ducks have long, narrow bills. These ducks eat larvae *(LARH vee),* the wormlike stage of newly hatched insects. The ducks use their bills to reach between river rocks to get the larvae.

Torrent ducks

What Are Sea Parrots?

Puffins have bright orange beaks—just like some parrots. And since puffins live by the sea, they are sometimes called sea parrots.

Puffins are excellent swimmers and divers. They spend most of their time on the water, swimming around and diving for fish and squid. They use their wings as flippers for swimming underwater.

Puffins are very social birds. They form flocks with thousands of members. Puffins often gather in small groups on rocks and cliff ledges. When a puffin lands, it greets the group with slightly raised wings. This greeting may let the others know that the bird means no harm.

Horned puffins

Which Swimming Birds Have Blue Feet?

Blue-footed boobies do! These swimming birds like to show off their feet, too. And who can blame them? Their blue feet really stand out!

Blue-footed boobies put their feet to good use. A male displays his feet during courtship. He holds up one foot at a time while arching his back. He then hops from one foot to the other. He wants to make sure the female gets a good look at both his feet!

Once the male has the female's attention, the courtship dance continues. The male whistles and the female honks as both boobies sky-point and strut.

Blue-footed boobies are very good divers. They fly high above the water looking for prey. When they spot food, such as fish and squid, they dive straight down. If they catch their prey, they bring it back to the surface to eat it.

Blue-footed booby

Who Likes a Good Laugh?

Loons have loud calls. Their calls sound like strange laughter. Some people even think the calls make a loon sound as if it's crazy!

A loon is a large, heavy bird that weighs about 9 pounds (4 kilograms). Its legs are so far back on its body that it has trouble walking. When a loon does walk, it seems to crawl on its belly. But having feet so far back helps a loon to swim and dive. Loons can swim underwater and can dive down to depths over 150 feet (45 meters).

Loons use their long, narrow bills to catch fish. They also use their bills to defend themselves. Loons are pretty tough. Just ask a fox or a young bear. Loons sometimes frighten off their enemies by striking with their sharp bills. Other times, loons sink down below the surface of the water to avoid danger.

Common loon

Who Takes Its Young Diving?

When a grebe goes for a swim, it often takes its young along for the ride. This is also true of other swimming birds. But scientists think that grebes are the only birds that take their young diving.

Newly hatched grebes may have to wait weeks before being able to dive well. When a parent is diving for food, young grebes may climb up under the parent's wings to go along for the dive. Grebes eat small fish, insects, snails, and shrimp.

Grebes are unlike other swimming birds in that they do not have webbed feet. Instead, each toe has a flap of skin that sticks out on one side. When a grebe swims, the flaps open. Each toe looks like a tiny paddle.

Great crested grebe

Can Storm-Petrels Really Walk on Water?

Storm-petrels seem to walk on water when they fly. Most petrels fly close to the water when they look for food. Their feet dip into the water or pat across the surface. This makes it look as if the birds are walking on water!

Storm-petrels are very tiny birds. They are so tiny that you could hold one in your hand. A storm-petrel may weigh as little as 1 ounce (30 grams). A bird so light in weight needs to be careful in strong winds. That may be why storm-petrels fly close to the surface of the water.

Storm-petrels do not come ashore often. When they do, it is usually to breed and to lay eggs. Storm-petrels often build little nests underground. Being underground protects them from many enemies.

Storm-petrel

Are Swimming Birds in Danger?

Yes, some swimming birds are in danger. But over the years, people have made great progress in protecting our wildlife. Today, many swimming birds that were once in danger are increasing in numbers.

During the 1800's and early 1900's, many birds were hunted for their meat and feathers. Trumpeter swans were greatly overhunted. It is believed that fewer than 70 swans were left in the United States in 1933.

Since that time, laws have been passed to protect birds and their habitats. One law, passed in 1934, is known as the Duck Stamp Act. Each year, a new stamp is issued that hunters must buy. The money raised is used to buy land and set up wildlife refuges. Today, because of laws like the Duck Stamp Act, there are about 16,000 trumpeter swans.

Trumpeter swans

Swimming Bird Fun Facts

→ Some swans often swim with one of their feet held over their backs. Some people think that this helps the swans keep cool.

→ About 400 species of birds can swim! That includes pelicans, gulls, and coots.

→ Eider "farms" actually contain wild eiders that visit the same nesting sites each year.

→ Long ago in England, only royalty could own mute swans. A Royal Swan Master kept track of the swans.

→ Cygnets that live in cold climates get their feathers earlier than other swans do. They need to be able to migrate before winter comes.

→ Loons and a few other birds that dive have solid bones. Loons are also able to let air out of their air sacs. This helps them sink.

→ A trumpeter swan may have a wingspan over 7 feet (2 meters) long.

Glossary

bill The hard part of a bird's jaws.

cob A male swan.

crest A tuft of feathers on a bird's head.

cygnet A young swan.

dabbler A swimming bird that eats water plants.

display To show off to please or attract a mate.

down Soft feathers.

drake A male duck.

duckling A young duck.

forage To search for food.

incubate To sit on eggs to make them warm enough to hatch.

larvae The newly hatched and wormlike offspring of insects.

migrate To move from one region to another, especially at a particular time of year.

molt To lose fur, skin, or another body covering before getting a new one.

pen A female swan.

preen To clean or care for the feathers with the beak.

refuge An area protected from danger or trouble.

sky-point To display by spreading the wings and pointing the bill toward the sky.

territory The place that animals keep for themselves only.

trachea The windpipe.

upend To reach underwater to feed by raising the tail into the air.

V-formation A V-shaped pattern formed by migrating birds.

waterproof Keeping water out.

wildlife refuge A place set aside to protect animals.

Index

(**Boldface** indicates a photo, map, or illustration.)

Picture Acknowledgments: Front & Back Cover: © Frank Kramer, Bruce Coleman Inc.; © Wayne Lankinen, Bruce Coleman Collection © Leonard Lee Rue III © Jeff Lepore, Photo Researchers; © Mary Plage, Bruce Coleman Collection.

© A.W. Ambler, Photo Researchers 11; © Jack A. Barrie, Bruce Coleman Inc. 31; © Erwin & Peggy Bauer, Bruce Coleman Inc. 39; © Jane Burton, Bruce Coleman Inc. 5, 35; © Tui DeRoy, Bruce Coleman Inc. 59; © Don Enger, Animals Animals 27; © F. Erize, Bruce Coleman Inc. 49; © Bob Glover, Bruce Coleman Collection, 15; © IFA from Bruce Coleman Inc. 23; © Frank Kramer, Bruce Coleman Inc. 3, 5, 13, 17; © Gordon Langsbury, Bruce Coleman Inc. 45; © Wayne Lankinen, Bruce Coleman Collection 33, 55; © Jess R. Lee, Photo Researchers 61; © Leonard Lee Rue III 41; © Jeff Lepore, Photo Researchers 4, 51; © George McCarthy, Bruce Coleman Collection 43; © Tero Niemi, Bruce Coleman Collection 57; © Mary Plage, Bruce Coleman Collection 53; © Hans Reinhard, Bruce Coleman Inc. 7, 21; © Kim Taylor, Bruce Coleman Collection 25; © Roger Tidman, Photo Researchers 47; © Frank S. Todd, EcoCepts International 19; © K. Westerkov/OSF from Animals Animals 29; © Edward F. Wolff, Animals Animals 37

Illustrations: WORLD BOOK illustration by Karen Donica 9, 62.

Swimming Bird Classification

Scientists classify animals by placing them into groups. The animal kingdom is a group that contains all the world's animals. Phylum, class, order, and family are smaller groups. Each phylum contains many classes. A class contains orders, and a family contains individual species. Each species also has its own scientific name. Here is how the animals in this book fit in to this system.

Animals with backbones and their relatives (Phylum Chordata)

Birds (Class Aves)

Ducks, Geese, Swans, and their relatives (Order Anseriformes)

Ducks, Geese, Swans (Family Anatidae)

African pygmy goose	*Nettapus auritus*
Barnacle goose	*Branta leucopsis*
Black swan	*Cygnus atratus*
Black-necked swan	*Cygnus melanocorypha*
Canada goose	*Branta canadensis*
Common eider	*Somateria mollissima*
Cotton pygmy goose	*Nettapus coromandelianus*
Greater white-fronted goose	*Anser albifrons*
Green pygmy goose	*Nettapus pulchellus*
Hooded merganser	*Lophodytes cucullatus*
King eider	*Somateria spectabilis*
Mallard	*Anas platyrhynchos*
Mandarin duck	*Aix galericulata*
Mute swan	*Cygnus olor*
Torrent duck	*Merganetta armata*
Tundra (whistling) swan	*Cygnus columbianus*
Trumpeter swan	*Cygnus buccinator*
Whooper swan	*Cygnus cygnus*

Marsh birds (Order Gruiformes)

Coots and their relatives (Family Rallidae)

Shorebirds, wading birds, and their relatives (Order Ciconiiformes)

Boobies and their relatives (Family Sulidae)

Blue-footed booby	*Sula nebouxii*

Grebes (Family Podicipedidae)

Great-crested grebe	*Podiceps cristatus*

Gulls, Puffins, and their relatives (Family Laridae)

Horned puffin	*Fratercula corniculata*

Loons (Family Gaviidae)

Common loon	*Gavia immer*

Pelicans (Family Pelecanidae)

Storm-petrels and their relatives (Family Procellariidae)